P9-DSZ-837

A RECOMMITMENT
TO AMERICA

I Pledge Allegiance

D. K. WEBB
DESIGN BY LINDEE LOVELAND

Our purpose at Howard Publishing is to:

- *Increase faith* in the hearts of growing Christians
- *Inspire holiness* in the lives of believers
- *Instill hope* in the hearts of struggling people everywhere

Because He's coming again!

Published by Howard Publishing Co., Inc.
3117 North 7th Street, West Monroe, Louisiana 71291-2227

02 03 04 05 06 07 08 09 10 11 10 9 8 7 6 5 4 3

Interior design by LinDee Loveland
Edited by Philis Boultinghouse

ISBN: 1-58229-254-X

contents

I pledge allegiance to the flag
of the United States of America
and to the Republic
for which it stands,
one Nation under God,
indivisible,
with liberty and justice
for all.

introduction

Thirty-one words... We learned them as kids when we were too small and too naive to understand them. We simply committed them to memory with no regard for their significance. We recited them morning after morning, year after year, never realizing the price that the proud revolutionists paid to make them real and the price our brave contemporaries would pay to *keep* them real. We've become so familiar with them that we seldom stop to consider what they should mean to us now...now that we're grown...now that we are the ones responsible for sustaining their legacy.

Whether we were aware of it or not, these thirty-one words carved out a place in our hearts—in the shape of a true patriot: a lover of liberty, a defender of faith, a promoter of unity, a champion of peace, a protector of democracy, and a guardian of all things sacred to life.

One morning recently, I paused in the midst of my busy routine to reflect on these thirty-one words. I was stunned at the emotions that stirred within me as I sat in respectful contemplation of not only these thirty-one words but of the wealth of history that lay behind them. Before I knew it, I found myself wanting to stand with my hand over my heart and recite them aloud with a renewed commitment to America—past, present, and future. And I did.

Perhaps it's time we all recommit to America—to her values, her traditions, her history, her heritage, her majesty, her nobility, her compassion, her humility, and her holy awe. Regardless of our party preference or political stance, regardless of which presidential candidate we supported or which amendments we opposed, we are—in all of our diversity—one people with one heart and one mind. We are the benefactors and beneficiaries of a powerful democracy—the strongest republic in the civilized world. We are the most liberated, most prosperous, and most blessed people on the face of the earth. And we owe it all to a sovereign God, to our American citizenship, and in part, to these thirty-one words.

Do yourself a favor. Do all of us a favor. Take the time right now to reflect on these thirty-one words and allow them to take root in your mind and heart. It is highly likely that your patriotism will be reaffirmed and your passion for this country reignited as you consider the thirty-one words you learned in elementary school.

What thirty-one words? You know them. I'll say the first three, and you can take it from there—the last twenty-eight are a piece of cake!

I pledge allegiance…
to the flag
of the United States of America
and to the Republic
for which it stands,
one Nation
under God,
indivisible,
with liberty
and justice
for all.

I

I

I pledge allegiance…

I pledge allegiance…

I…

The call to commitment is an extremely radical, very personal call to rally around the cause of freedom, to consciously individuate my commitment at the very core of my identity.

I… A *very* personal pronoun.

Not *we*, not *you*, not *they*…but *I*.

I is in the first person singular. And how appropriate that the first word in the pledge of commitment that I recite to my country, to my flag, is in the first person singular.

The first person I must consider in honoring this country's legacy of faith and freedom is *me*. *I* am singularly responsible for my contribution to our integrity and dignity. *I* alone am accountable for my participation in our heritage of hope and prosperity. *I* solely am answerable for my diligence in matters

of loyalty and honor. *I* am individually liable for protecting the rights of others, for promoting the freedom of us all. *I* am the first person I hold responsible for supporting our government, for applauding our patriots, for honoring our heroes, and for joining their ranks.

It is *I* that I must face when it comes to loving mercy, doing justice, and living with integrity. I must first face *myself* by owning my courage or admitting my need of it, by extending my willingness or confessing my want of it, by living up to my commitment or confronting my lack of it. It all begins right here—with *me*.

I must revisit *my* allegiance to this great nation.

I alone. A *very* personal way to begin.

The strength of our numbers begins with the solitary commitment of each individual—each patriot—determining in his or her heart to become an integral part of something bigger than self. As *I* join ranks with the myriad fellow Americans who pledge alongside me a mutual trust, *I* become a part of the greater *we*, the people of these United States of America.

I…

pledge

pledge

What brilliance! Someone in 1892 suggested that school children recite this vow of allegiance on some long-forgotten occasion. Who would have thought this one-time recital would launch a patriotic tradition that would become a part of the very fiber of the lives of millions of young Americans destined to become the grateful and responsible citizens of the free world?

It was a great service to us that we, as children, learned to recite this pledge while so young and impressionable. As Americans, we harbor within our hearts cherished and vivid memories of this first official act of the school day. Standing beside our desks in our classrooms, with freshly scrubbed faces, hands pressed over our hearts, and newly awakened eyes intent upon the flag, we pledged our allegiance. With a respect and awe we didn't nearly comprehend, we made a promise to the flag that hung from some wall, beside some chalkboard, in some schoolroom, in some town—all across the United States.

In resounding unison, our young voices raised the standard that has been etched upon our lives as a critical part of our great heritage—down the halls, across the street, over the mountains, through the valleys, across the fields, echoing across the vast landscape of our liberty in a united posture of loyalty. Our small minds could not even begin to fathom the implications of the pledge we were making. There upon the freshly turned soil of our tender hearts was engraved an indelible impression of our integrity—a solemn vow—a promise that we would be faithful to our flag, yes even unto death, if death it did require.

With all the inherent blessings of the daily training of our young minds, we risked becoming desensitized to the sobering reality of our solemn vow by over-familiarizing ourselves through our daily verbal cadence. Have we become numb to the fact that from our earliest beginnings we agreed to lay down our lives to embrace an unwavering commitment, a sacred covenant—not to a symbol of freedom but to a free people—to each other, to those with whom we live and work, to the very ones we love?

Whether in the hour of our greatest trial or in the moment-by-moment minutiae of our daily routine, we, the people, must never turn back from our pledge. We must revive our passion and renew our oath so that we live out our days in the dignity and honor of our heritage.

> *Fourscore and seven years ago our fathers brought forth upon this continent a new nation, conceived in liberty.... It is for us, the living,...to be dedicated here to the unfinished work which they who fought here have thus far so nobly advanced. It is...for us to be here dedicated to the great task remaining before us, that from these honored dead we take increased devotion to that cause for which they gave the last full measure of devotion; that we here highly resolve that these dead shall not have died in vain; that this nation, under God, shall have a new birth of freedom, and that government of the people, by the people, and for the people, shall not perish from the earth.*
>
> ABRAHAM LINCOLN'S "GETTYSBURG ADDRESS"

I do personally, solemnly vow...

allegian

allegiance

I do personally, solemnly vow my allegiance—my *loyalty*, my *fidelity*.

The word *allegiance* stirs a nobler strain within us than we esteem ourselves capable of fleshing out. We conjure up images of soldiers and saints whose spirits shine like stars, ignited with zeal and infused with passion, persevering under conditions so adverse and in a darkness so deep that the soul is bowed under its weight, yet they march on. Heroes. Champions of courage.

For what cause would men and women beg the opportunity to prove their devotion—a cause that exists so close to the edge of tyranny that it would put their very lives at stake? What cause but freedom?

We, therefore, the representatives of the United States of America,...appealing to the Supreme Judge of the World for the Rectitude of our Intentions, do, in the Name and by Authority of the good People of these Colonies, solemnly Publish and Declare, That these United Colonies are, and of Right ought to be, Free and Independent States.... And for the support of this declaration, with a firm reliance on the protection of Divine Providence, we mutually pledge to each other our lives, our fortunes, and our sacred honor.

THE DECLARATION OF INDEPENDENCE

This is the allegiance avowed: my life, my fortune, my sacred honor.

Pay for freedom at such a price as this?

Not if freedom claims to reign within the restraints of a sovereignty so cruel that it severs its people from a reasonable pursuit of faith and fulfillment.

Not if freedom alleges to exist within the confines of a government so rigid that it suffocates the innovation and industry of its greatest minds.

Not if freedom purports to prevail within a prison of oppression by rulers so lacking in compassion that they refuse to protect their own from their undignified assaults.

Not if freedom professes to triumph within the gridlock of a power so abusive that the sovereign right, the free will, and the desires of the heart are beaten out of its constituents by poverty, hunger, and desperation.

But *this* is America! The land of opportunity and abundance. Is the price of life too great to pay for a freedom such as ours? Not if living—*really* living—finds its definition in *freedom*. But what value is life if not given in pledge and pursuit of living in earnest?

What treasure has man without opportunity? What fortune have we without the freedom to obtain it? What fulfillment in life, what enjoyment, what adventure if not the liberty to pursue it? What honor without the courage of our convictions on behalf of one another? We do not live in the spirit of our Creator if we exist without freedom.

This allegiance, this loyalty, this devotion inspires in us an unsuspected nobility. We may be called upon to become heroes, not by choice, but by fidelity.

I do personally, solemnly vow my life, my loyalty, and my sacred honor…

to the flag

Old Glory! Her majestic train has waved faithfully over us in grace and grandeur all of our lives, signaling to any curious onlooker, any foreign power, any eye of treason that she is keeping watch over the sacred trust of her loyal patrons with undying devotion.

Oh! Say, can you see, by the dawn's early light,
What so proudly we hailed at the twilight's last gleaming?

Surely none of us can recall the first time our eyes beheld the ensign of our patriotism. The image exists as such an integral part of our national identity that we could no sooner remember its introduction than we could remember the first time we saw the reflection of our own faces.

Whose broad stripes and bright stars, thro' the perilous fight,
O'er the ramparts we watched were so gallantly streaming?

She represents the visage of glory, the strength and passion of the American way of life. Resilient, radical, concise, compelling, powerful, profound, efficient, energetic, simplistic, stately—incredibly inspiring. Never static, the herald of our country's progress and prosperity remained in a state of healthy flux for more than two hundred years—from the original thirteen stars to the present fifty.

Congress said of the star-spangled standard, *"RESOLVED: that the flag of the United States be thirteen stripes…that the Union be thirteen stars…representing a new constellation."* And she, the resplendent glory of the governmental galaxy, exudes her pride in articulate dignity and indomitable strength. Her stellar brilliance stands head and shoulders above the banners of all other republics.

And the rockets' red glare, the bombs bursting in air,
Gave proof thro' the night that our flag was still there.

Publishing the unbridled energy and exuberance of her constituents, our emblem evokes an emotional response so intense there exists no room for indifference in the hearts of people. Men either love her or loathe her. She is either adored or abhorred. Revered or despised. Strutted or spit upon. The firebrand of freedom inflames the passions of statesmen and renegades alike. But we, the people, salute her as the impregnable symbol of life, liberty, and the pursuit of happiness.

Oh! Say, does that star-spangled banner yet wave
O'er the land of the free and the home of the brave!

Our careful code for handling her demonstrates our lofty esteem. We "run her up the flagpole" briskly at dawn, then retrieve her slowly and reverently at dusk. We observe a solemn salute whether at sporting events or political gatherings. We drape our coffins with her dignified robes as a last tribute to a worthy life and sing to her standard in passionate strains at the top of our lungs. We weep when she's reared among the ruins of national tragedy or personal triumph. Dignified men uncover their heads in obeisance, and ragamuffins stand at attention when she passes by. We rally to her side when hoisted in the face of war or elevated in reverent recognition of peace. We cherish her stately message in our hearts and clasp our hands over our bosoms to retain her indelible image there.

I do personally, solemnly vow my life, my loyalty, and my sacred honor to the ultimate and indiscriminate trophy of our blood-bought freedom—the ensign of democracy that billows protectively over the tremor of the feeble and calls to the fore the courage of the brave at heart.

of the
United States

of the United States of America

They tell us, Sir, that we are weak—unable to cope with so formidable an adversary. But when shall we be stronger? Will it be the next week, or the next year?... Shall we gather strength by irresolution and inaction?... Sir, we are not weak, if we make a proper use of those means which the God of nature hath placed in our power.

PATRICK HENRY, "THE WAR INEVITABLE"

The United States—our identity from the inside, out.

America—our identity from the outside, in.

We, the people, are a powerfully united entity—and the entire civilized world recognizes the strength of our solidarity. Whether applauded or despised, our unity is anything but ignored.

of America

In the normal course of events, presidents come to this chamber to report on the state of the Union. Tonight, no such report is needed. It has already been delivered by the American people.... My fellow citizens, for the last nine days, the entire world has seen for itself the state of our Union—and it is strong.

GEORGE W. BUSH

Our history looks back along a brilliant trail blazed by compassionate concern for men and women as individuals and their communities as essential integers. We are united on a personal level—in families and on teams; on a religious level—in churches and communities of common belief; on a local level—in subdivisions and neighborhoods; on the regional level—in towns, cities, and states; and on the national level—as an assembled whole.

We are a nation fitted together state by state, like a massive jigsaw puzzle, yet with genuine respect for the autonomy of each province and authentic regard for the integrity of representative government.

We are one continuous and contiguous whole, consolidated by common goals and mutually beneficial aspirations. We are of one heart and mind, blending the rivulets of our intellectual powers and our most effectual sentiments into one consummate river of life, liberty, and love for our fellowman.

We have learned the value of acting in concert toward a common end. We have brought to fruition our brightest prospects and realized our greatest potential by mutual participation in our unabridged hopes and our unedited dreams. The strength of our affinity lies most tightly trussed in our pervasive love of freedom.

We, the people, are one; and we are free.

But our freedom is only half of our concern, for this is America! Recognized by our foreign allies as the most compassionate people on the earth, we not only take a stand for our own liberty, but we willingly lay down our lives on behalf of the freedom of all people everywhere.

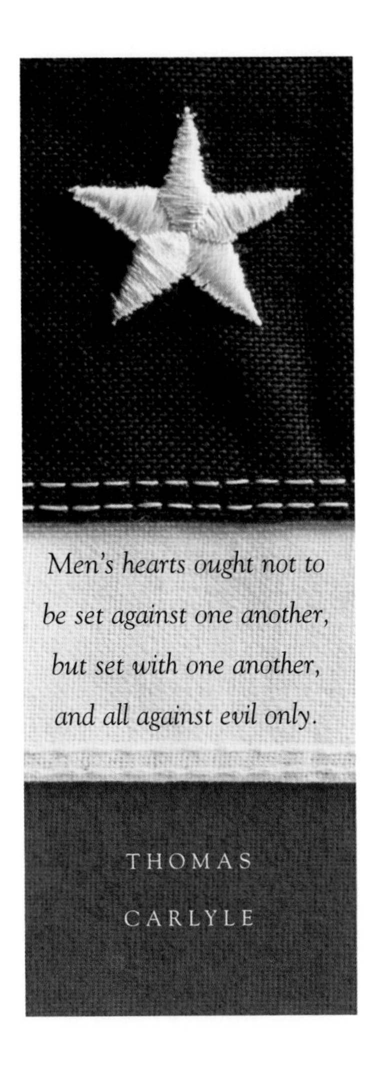
Men's hearts ought not to be set against one another, but set with one another, and all against evil only.

THOMAS CARLYLE

We the People
of the United States,
insure domestic Tranquility, provide for the common defence, promote the general
and our Posterity, do ordain and establish this Constitution for the United States of
Article I
and to the

and to the Republic

We the people of the United States, in order to form a more perfect union...do ordain and establish this Constitution for the United States of America.

THE PREAMBLE OF THE CONSTITUTION OF THE UNITED STATES

It was an outrageous risk our founding fathers ventured, staking the strength of the government and the fiber of our freedom upon the commitment and integrity of our responsible selection. We own the invaluable right to elect ordinary men and women to positions of extraordinary responsibility within our legislature. And we have the ultimate right to refuse to participate in that election as well.

Our constitutional government derives a great portion of its strength and resilience from the unselfish sense of duty of every American citizen to the legislative processes. Loyalty to our government must surely begin with our commitment to participate in the representative processes that have been put in place. When people can afford to be casual about their suffrage, they have reached the point of indifference that takes for granted the freedoms that other, nobler men laid down their lives to ensure. Will we abdicate our voice in government by our lack of concern and our love of convenience?

How dare we boast of our willingness to rally around a war-worn banner in the heat of battle when we care so little about our blood-bought freedom that we don't even fight traffic to exercise our freedom at the polls? Surely we wouldn't claim an eagerness to go across the sea to fight for freedom when we won't even go across the street to vote.

When our voices are silenced by our own lack of initiative and conviction or muted by apathy and self-centered pursuits, then we have abandoned our solemn vow of loyalty. We have forsaken the right to freedom. We have become parasites upon the lives of true patriots.

Every American must care enough to protect and defend the Republic, our democracy, from the most insidious enemy of all—our own indifference! Where captive hearts cry out for compassionate leaders, they envision a deeply cherished democracy whose citizens hold in the highest esteem their right of choice, their freedom of expression.

Norman Cousins once said, "In a democracy, the individual enjoys not only the ultimate power but carries the ultimate responsibility." And that ultimate responsibility is fleshed out in the discipline and diligence of those who hold in proper regard the power of choice, the essential influence of each voice. We govern ourselves rightly when we refuse to indulge ourselves in the mediocrity of convenience and the apathy of indifference. We uphold and support our compatriots by exercising due diligence in matters of the heart, the state, and the nation.

Let us be done with the incompetent negligence and the reckless unconcern of a dispassionate disposition. Let us be finished with lukewarm commitments and a sluggard's lack of fervor. May we exchange shrugs of insensitivity and nods of nonchalance for hearts of ardent zeal, attitudes of eager devotion, and spirits of deep conviction. Let us—everyone—join the passionate ranks of the bloodstained Republic with new resolve, convinced that each person's view, each voice, and each solemn vow are our reasonable and responsible contributions.

for which

for which it stands

Yesterday, December 7, 1941—a date which will live in infamy—the United States of America was suddenly and deliberately attacked by naval and air forces of the Empire of Japan.... With confidence in our armed forces, with the unbounding determination of our people, we will gain the inevitable triumph, so help us God!

FRANKLIN D. ROOSEVELT

On February 23, 1945, atop Mount Suribachi, six marines bent shoulder to shoulder to raise Old Glory in splendid array over the island of Iwo Jima, signaling the presence of American forces on site. Up through the rubble on the top of the volcano they had affectionately dubbed "Hot Rock," they hoisted a piece of iron drainage pipe—weighing over one hundred pounds—with the Stars and Stripes attached and flapping valiantly in the wind. Cheers erupted from the troops below as hope filled their hearts and reignited their courage. The photograph of that incident lives in our memories forever.

Fifty-six years later…

On September the 11th, enemies of freedom committed an act of war against our country. Americans have known wars—but for the past 136 years, they have been wars on foreign soil, except for one Sunday in 1941. Americans have known the casualties of war—but not at the center of a great city on a peaceful morning. Americans have known surprise attacks—but never before on thousands of civilians. All of this was brought upon us in a single day—and night fell on a different world, a world where freedom itself is under attack…. Great harm has been done to us. We have suffered great loss. And in our grief and anger we have found our mission and our moment. Freedom and fear are at war. The advance of human freedom—the great achievement of our time and the great hope of every time—now depends on us. Our nation—this generation—will lift a dark threat of violence from our people and our future. We will rally the world to this cause by our efforts, by our courage. We will not tire, we will not falter, and we will not fail.

GEORGE W. BUSH

On September 11, 2001, atop the fallen World Trade Center in New York, three brave firemen bent shoulder to shoulder to raise Old Glory in splendid array over the island of Manhattan, signaling the presence of the American people on site in full force. Up through the rubble of the buildings we had affectionately dubbed the "Twin Towers," they hoisted a flag—confiscated from a yacht docked nearby—in the aftermath of a terrorist attack. The Stars and Stripes, and all that she

symbolizes, stood in stark contrast to the travesty that surrounded. Tears streamed down the faces of a nation, as hope filled our hearts and reignited our courage. The sight of that incident lives in our memories forever.

The nine men who raised our flag on these two historical occasions demonstrated what it means to stand: to proclaim, insist, hold on, maintain, profess, assert, persist, and affirm that what we believe is worth believing. Within the hearts of us all, we have taken a solemn vow to do what these men did, to affirm that for which our Republic stands. The democracy that governs us is a "government of the people, by the people, and for the people." It is up to us, as the people, to stand with her.

Whether in the immortalized grip of a battle-worn marine battalion on Iwo Jima or draped over the shards of the Pentagon in Washington, D.C., or raised by the soot-stained hands of firemen in the ruins of Manhattan, Old Glory beckons to the spirits of free men and women from coast to coast to rally to the legacy of our liberty.

I do personally, solemnly vow my life, my loyalty, and my sacred honor to the ultimate and indiscriminate trophy of our blood-bought freedom—the ensign of democracy—that billows protectively over the tremor of the feeble and calls to the fore the courage of the brave at heart. I promise my faithfulness, as well, to the people of these United States: inseparable in heart, impartial in judgment, intolerant of tyranny, and integrated in freedom.

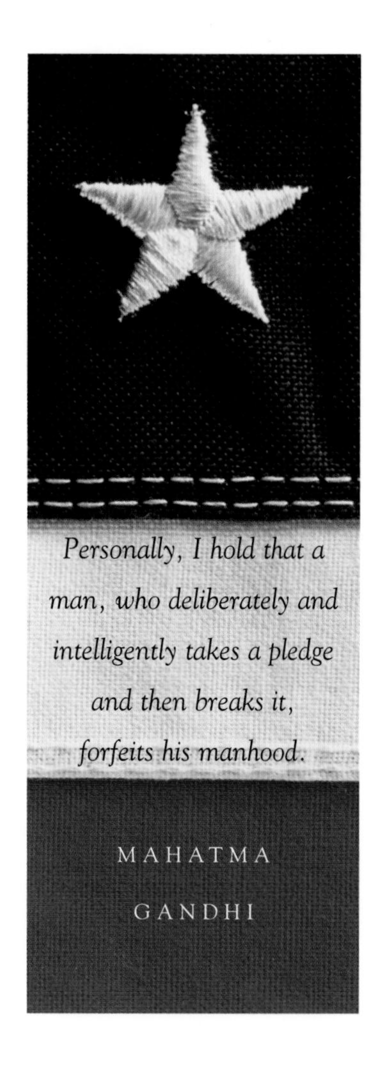

one Nation
LEMONADE
ICE COLD
ONLY 2¢
ICE
COLD
2¢
California

one Nation

We hold these truths to be self-evident: that all men are created equal, that they are endowed by their Creator with certain inalienable rights, that among these are life, liberty, and the pursuit of happiness.

THE DECLARATION OF INDEPENDENCE

What a statement! Founded upon the principles of equality, freedom, democracy, opportunity, and free enterprise, our forefathers pioneered for us what the entire world now knows as "The American Dream." Many men laid down their lives to ensure that the dream would come true. Countless women and children lost their lovers and providers in pursuit of that ideal. And we, the sometimes careless citizens of this nation's abundance, the passive patrons of this country's legacy, must rally to recognize our blessings and express our devotion in order to keep the dream alive—a vibrant hope dawning on the horizons of future generations.

The spirit of those engaged in the fight for independence included a strong conviction regarding government by the people. While the memories of a heavy-handed despotism remained fresh in their minds and the open wounds of oppression still oozed the blood of the patriots, the American people were appropriately unified in a fervent and grateful participation in national affairs. To this very day, we maintain the right to have an active voice in our government, and it is incumbent upon us still to exercise our influence and integrity in legislative matters. May we never be too far removed from the memory of our desperate beginnings to appreciate the unity that is ours to honor, sustain, and perpetuate.

This nation is as diverse in landscape as in populace! From the warm, salty surf licking the beaches of Florida to the frigid, ice-encrusted borders of Alaska; from the sharp, brisk New England pace to the genteel and leisurely Southern grace, Americans are free to express their individuality in incredibly colorful ways. Yet with all of our diversity, we are intensely of one heart and mind. And when tested by tragedy, terrorism, or war; when threatened by invasive outsiders; or when the voice of betrayal from a false-hearted treasonist assaults our ears, we stand as a very present and unified whole to thwart any perpetrator of injustice, to disarm any menace to freedom.

The composers of our Constitution committed an act of outright political genius. As a result, we have a living, breathing document of government—a document embedded with a resilience that allows for the growth and expansion of a progressive nation without compromising its original splendor and strength. And as the constituents of such constitutional government, we exercise an incredible independence and individuality within the framework of profound unity.

We are the people of a great nation, a great democracy, and a great liberty; and we are one. This lush landscape we call America is the inheritance of the children of independence. But far greater than that, our unity is the legacy of the devoted champions of our freedom.

under

under God

The phrase "under God" was added to the Pledge by Congress in 1954.

> *In this way we are reaffirming the transcendence of religious faith in America's heritage and future; in this way we shall constantly strengthen those spiritual weapons which forever will be our country's most powerful resource in peace and war.*
>
> DWIGHT D. EISENHOWER

Mine eyes have seen the glory
of the coming of the Lord...

We are a nation whose foundation was built upon faith and religious freedom. We salute our democracy, our flag, and the highest officials in our land; however, our spirits ultimately bow in reverent awe before the Sovereign Ruler of the universe.

It would be peculiarly improper to omit in this first official act my fervent supplications to that Almighty Being who rules over the universe, who presides in the councils of nations, and whose providential aids can supply every human defect, that His benediction may consecrate to the liberties and happiness of the people of the United States.... No people can be bound to acknowledge and adore the Invisible Hand which conducts the affairs of men more than those of the United States. Every step by which they have advanced to the character of an independent nation seems to have been distinguished by some token of providential agency.

GEORGE WASHINGTON

And though we, in times of peace, disagree and engage in loud debate about whether to express our faith in the public arena or whether to pray in public schools, we all rally in the Great Throne Room of the Almighty when tragedy strikes and our hearts are humbled in fear.

He is trampling out the vintage
where the grapes of wrath are stored...

The hearts of the American people cry out to the heavens when some of our sons and daughters are taken hostage in airplanes navigating suicide missions of terror and others are marched off to war. Where will we turn but to the only One who can deliver us from the assault of evil?

He hath loosed the fateful lightning
of His terrible swift sword;
His truth is marching on…

As we have been assured, neither death nor life, nor angels nor principalities nor powers, nor things present nor things to come, nor height nor depth, can separate us from God's love. May He bless the souls of the departed. May He comfort our own. And may He always guide our country. God bless America.

GEORGE W. BUSH

He has sounded forth the trumpet
that shall never sound retreat…

The song "God Bless America" echoes through our land: in Congress, on the steps of the Capital, in stadiums, in churches, on baseball fields, in concert

halls, in P.T.O. meetings, on radio, on television, in the hearts and on the lips of every American when our freedom is so violently attacked. We are incredulous at any assault on our liberty, on our economy, and on our lives. But we are not surprised when that assault sends us to our knees in prayer.

He is sifting out the hearts of men
before His judgment seat…

Three millions of People, armed in the holy cause of liberty, and in such a country as that which we possess, are invincible by any force which our enemy can send against us. Beside, Sir, we shall not fight our battles alone. There is a just God who presides over the destinies of Nations, and who will raise up friends to fight our battles for us. The battle, Sir, is not to the strong alone; it is to the vigilant, the active, the brave.

PATRICK HENRY

O be swift, my soul, to answer Him,
be jubilant, my feet!
Our God is marching on.

We are the people, and we have a mighty God.

Glory, glory, hallelujah!
Glory, glory, hallelujah!
Glory, glory, hallelujah!
His truth is marching on.

For the eyes of the LORD move to and fro throughout the earth that He may strongly support those whose heart is completely His.

2 CHRONICLES 16:9

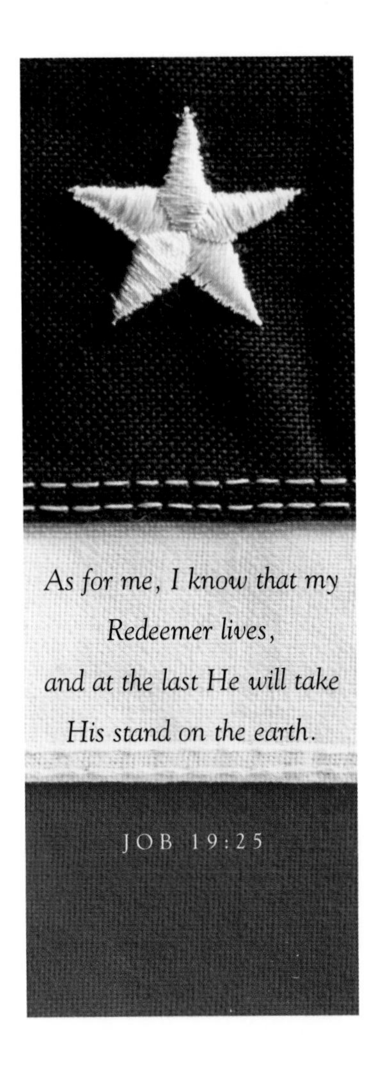

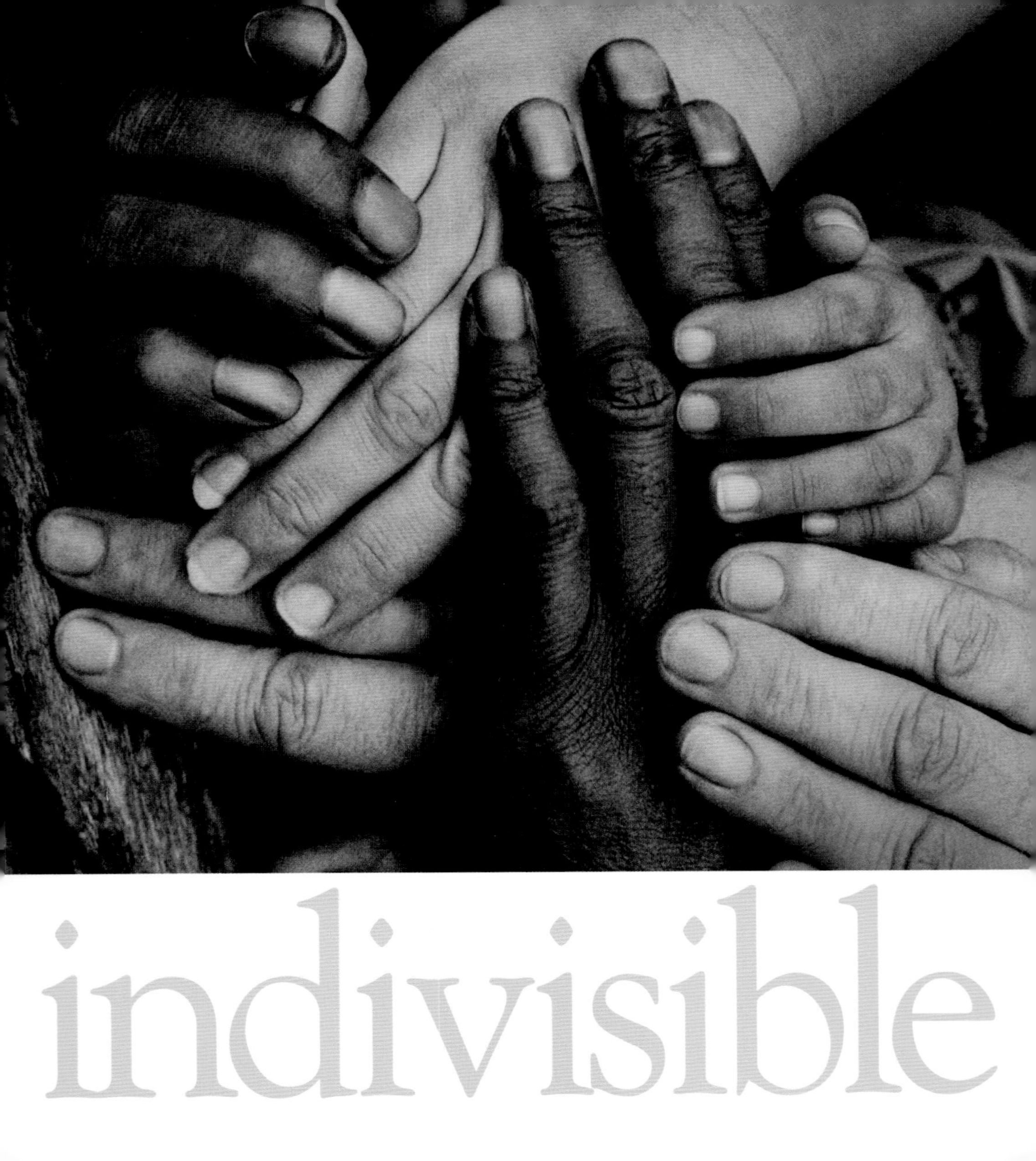
indivisible

indivisible

It is one thing to come together as one; it is quite another to *stay* together as one. We, the people of the United States of America, are bound together as one nation by a common thread of history, a common love of liberty, a common commitment to democracy, and a common bond of unity. But it will require an *uncommon* devotion to each other and to these ideals to maintain all that has been built for us on common ground.

The element of indivisibility isn't ours simply because the word is present in our national oath of allegiance. Contrarily, the strength of our oneness is dependent upon the integrity of our lives as the responsible citizens of a free nation. What makes us indissoluble is our individual resolve, on a day-by-day basis, to the principles that tied us together in the first place.

Let us do our duty in our shop or our kitchen, in the market, the street, the office, the school, the home, just as faithfully as if we stood in the front rank of some great battle, and knew that victory for mankind depended on our bravery, strength and skill. When we do that, the humblest of us will be serving in that great army which achieves the welfare of the world.

THEODORE PARKER

The enemies of our great nation have discovered, much to their shock and dismay, that acts of aggression committed against us will not destroy our unity. In fact, when attacked, we become more united, not less. We are not more *vulnerable* under assault, we are more *impenetrable*. Our fierce love of independence is actually a deeply rooted interdependence, for we know that we stand as one immovable and indestructible whole—*together*.

This inseparable and incorruptible quality depends upon our individual determination to uphold our integrity as a nation and to cling to the solidarity of our faith. We must return to our roots—our passion for freedom, for faith, and for independence. We must restore our patriotic fervor—our love of mankind, our love of God, and our devotion to democracy. And we must forge into our future with renewed commitment and resolve. This and this alone will ensure that we remain indivisible under the provision and protection of the Sovereign One.

I do personally, solemnly vow my life, my loyalty, and my sacred honor to the ultimate and indiscriminate trophy of our blood-bought freedom—the ensign of democracy—that billows protectively over the tremor of the feeble and calls to the fore the courage of the brave at heart. I promise my faithfulness, as well, to the people of these United States: inseparable in heart, impartial in judgment, intolerant of tyranny, and integrated in freedom. And I pledge my commitment to our unity—our oneness of heart, mind, and purpose.

with liberty

with liberty

It is in vain, Sir, to extenuate the matter. Gentlemen may cry, Peace, Peace!—but there is no peace. The war is actually begun! The next gale that sweeps from the North will bring to our ears the clash of resounding arms! Our brethren are already in the field! Why stand we here idle? What is it that Gentlemen wish? What would they have? Is life so dear, or peace so sweet, as to be purchased at the price of chains and slavery? Forbid it, Almighty God! I know not what course others may take; but as for me, give me liberty or give me death!

PATRICK HENRY, "THE WAR INEVITABLE"

Ah, liberty! The very word ignites the embers of our fierce independence, fanning into full flame the deepest passion that exists within the heart of the true patriot. The noble pilgrims of our ancient freedom would sooner grace the grave in dignity than bear the marks of bondage to some unprincipled despot. And so must we!

The cost of freedom is always high, but Americans have always paid it. And one path we shall never choose, and that is the path of surrender, or submission.

JOHN F. KENNEDY

By divine design, our immortal spirits were created with the capacity and the yearning to live unfettered! Free! We were born with the right to have autonomous dominion over our personal existence. We were created to exercise free will and virtuous living on a magnanimous scale. We are called to a higher purpose and a greater morality than the low living demonstrated by selfish people who destroy the dreams of their fellow man, who drive the desperate into deeper despair, who crush the cherished hopes of the living, who trample the sacred memories of the noble dead.

What light is to the eyes—what air is to the lungs—what love is to the heart, liberty is to the soul of man.

ROBERT GREEN INGERSOLL

Freedom as a philosophy sets one's feet upon the path of discipline, discretion, and decision; it holds firmly to the credo of compassion, conscience, and courage. Liberty—true liberty—springs from a heart of deep integrity, breathes life back into burdened souls, and strikes a mortal blow at the root of evil and duplicity.

Whether threatened by enemies without—the bondage of tyranny and terrorism—or taunted by enemies within—the insidious cancer of civil unrest—the cause of liberty lifts her radiant visage with courage and strength to face her foes. When evil invaders of a liberated republic—the dreadful opponents of independence—do deep-level violence to the spirits of a free people, we hear the clarion call to take up arms: the helmet of capable minds, the breastplate of honest hearts, the shield of industrious arms, the spear of skillful hands, the shodding of productive feet, and the chariot of swift and courageous action. As Cicero so poignantly stated, "Freedom suppressed and again regained bites with keener fangs than freedom never endangered." Free people embrace the fight to retain their inalienable right!

and

and justice

The forward progression of a strong and united nation keeps two elements marching in perfect cadence side by side: liberty and justice. Justice is that which keeps liberty pure. Daniel Webster said, "Justice is the ligament which holds civilized beings and civilized nations together."

We are a people who believe that our freedom is our entitlement as children of a sovereign God. We also believe that our liberty is ultimately our greatest responsibility. For in order to be truly free, we must live responsibly among other free agents, appropriating our freedom in unbiased and equitable regard for all.

Give me your tired, your poor, your huddled masses yearning to breathe free, the wretched refuse of your teeming shore. Send these, the homeless, tempest-tossed to me. I lift my lamp beside the golden door.

EMMA LAZARUS,
INSCRIBED ON THE STATUE OF LIBERTY

When a nation stands for justice, it stands for truth; for justice is, in effect, "truth in action" (Disraeli). And truth is the only reasonable and rational basis for maintaining freedom. When a nation fails to act upon injustice, people begin to lose their freedom bit by bit. The redress of wrong is essential to their confidence and security. And justice preserves and protects the people's well-being.

Tonight we are a country awakened to danger and called to defend freedom. Our grief has turned to anger, and anger to resolution. Whether we bring our enemies to justice, or bring justice to our enemies, justice will be done.... Be ready.... The hour is coming when America will act, and you will make us proud.

GEORGE W. BUSH

Justice begins in the heart with an unbiased and impartial measure of mercy. He who longs for justice must first learn to love mercy. Mercy thrives on understanding the nature of man: his frailties and his weaknesses. True justice takes into account the portfolio of a person's character in its larger context rather than in isolated snapshots of singular activity.

And justice requires courage, as well: the courage of our convictions as we mete out with fairness what is fitting and due in the best interests of all. We may adhere to a right system of belief, but until we are put to the ultimate test of adversity, we do not know the temper and fiber of our convictions. Justice follows through on what we perceive as truth.

> *In reality justice was...being concerned...not with the outward man, but with the inward, which is the true self and concernment of man: for the just man...sets in order his own inner life, and is his own master and his own law, and at peace with himself.*
>
> PLATO, "THE REPUBLIC"

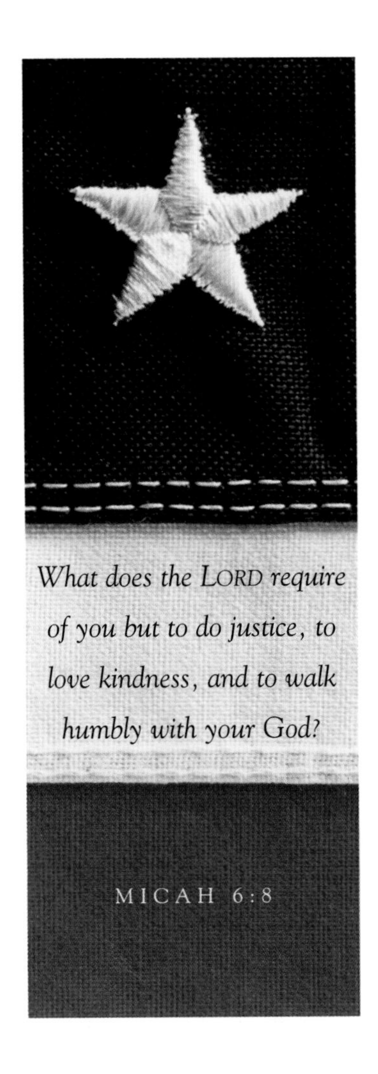

for all

For *all?*

For *all!*

For tiny babies just born, who sleep in innocence through the long night of freedom's fight. For old men who sit on porches—fondling tarnished medals adorned with faded, crumpled ribbons—remembering their battles as they watch younger patriots now bear arms. For the working class who labor day in and day out to advance a system of free enterprise. For old women who wipe the tears from the faces of the young as they sorrow over the fallen brave. For the young and idealistic who aspire to accomplish all the shattered dreams of all who have gone before. For the sick and the weak as well as the whole and the strong. For the uncertain and insecure as well as the confident and courageous.

for all

Our solemn vow of loyalty must further the cause of freedom and fairness for *all*.

We began in consideration of *I*. We end in consideration of *all*. Loyalty is a matter of commitment by the individual on behalf of *all*. Unity is a matter of individual purpose on behalf of *all*. Democracy is a matter of individual resolve on behalf of *all*. Freedom and justice are matters of individual dedication on behalf of *all*. And faith is a matter of individual consecration on behalf of the Almighty.

We are the people. We are *all* the people. We are *all* the people who pledge our patriotic allegiance to the star-spangled banner of freedom that waves above the greatest, most powerful, most prosperous, most compassionate, most liberated nation on earth. We are the people who vow loyalty to the democracy that exists in its noble imperfection to keep us *all* free. We *all* comprise one nation—a nation that owes its ultimate allegiance to the one God. And we *all* individually pledge our pursuit of liberty and justice for *all*.

We are Americans—the people—in passionate pursuit of life and freedom for *all*.

I *do personally, solemnly* VOW
my life, *my* loyalty, *and my sacred* honor
to the ultimate *and* indiscriminate *trophy of our* blood-bought *freedom*
—the ensign of democracy—
that billows protectively *over the tremor of the feeble*
and calls *to the fore the courage of the* brave *at heart.*
I *promise my* faithfulness,
as well, to the people *of these United States:*
inseparable *in heart,*
impartial *in judgment,*
intolerant *of tyranny,*
and integrated *in freedom.*
And I *pledge my commitment to our* unity,
our oneness *of heart, mind, and purpose—*forever
and for the sake of
us all.

I pledge allegiance to the flag
of the United States of America
and to the Republic
for which it stands,
one Nation
under God,
indivisible,
with liberty and justice
for all.